Bone Road

in word and image

John Brown's Mammoth Cash Grocery, c 1890s

Geraldine Mills

BONE ROAD

in word and image

ARLEN HOUSE

Bone Road
in word and image

is published in 2020 by
Arlen House
42 Grange Abbey Road
Baldoyle
Dublin D13 A0F3
Ireland
Phone: 00 353 86 8360236
arlenhouse@gmail.com

978–1–85132–244–2

International distribution
Syracuse University Press
621 Skytop Road, Suite 110
Syracuse
New York 13244–5290
Phone: 315–443–5534
email: supress@syr.edu

Typesetting by Arlen House

Cover artwork:
'The Crossing'
by Charlotte Kelly
is reproduced courtesy of the artist
www.charlottekelly.com

CONTENTS

The house on the corner of Water Street and Bowen,
Warren, Rhode Island, 1929

In memory of those who went and came back;
especially our sister Bernadette,
who died 22 May 2016

Great Sachem Massasoit's commemoration

INTRODUCTION

Growing up in the west of Ireland, I knew nothing about my maternal great-grandparents and their children, other than the fact that they emigrated from Belmullet to America and came back some time later. Then I heard of James Hack Tuke, discovered a ship's manifest with their names on it, received a Facebook request from an unknown cousin looking to make contact and suddenly their story came rushing up for air.

Belmullet was a 'margin land' with no road in or out of it until 1824. Concerned people venturing to trawl through this impoverished place were appalled by the conditions in which the people lived. It is where my ancestors could not eke out a living from the unforgiving terrain.

Mr Tuke, a Quaker, was born in 1819 in York, England, the seventh son of a prominent philanthropic Quaker family and tea merchant. It was at the request of the Quakers that he, a young man of 26 years, was first sent to Ireland to review the famine situation during the Great Hunger. Haunted by the scenes of destitution that he saw in the west, he recorded it all in his letter addressed to the

Central Relief Committee of the Society of Friends, *A Visit to Connaught in the Autumn of 1847*.

Returning to Ireland in the spring of 1880, he found that the people on the western seaboard were still living at subsistence level. The only solution he could see was assisted emigration.

He did his homework, visiting the US and Canada in 1880 to seek out the best places to send them, even meeting with the then president of the US, Rutherford Hayes, and the prime minister of Canada, Sir John McDonald. Gathering together a number of equally concerned people, they set up the Assisted Emigration Scheme under the Arrears Act and the fund, known as the 'Tuke Fund' was established in March 1882. Between that time and 1884, the fund supported approximately 6000 from Connemara and 3,300 from County Mayo to emigrate for a better life in America and Canada.

The scheme was voluntary, only whole families were considered and the poorest were given priority, saving them from the poorhouse. Other stipulations were that one of them had to be able to speak English, and some of the children old enough to work. By sending whole families, their holdings could be consolidated with those who stayed, easing the congestion and the burden on the land. To prevent overcrowding in the new world, they scattered the emigrants to as many as 80 destinations in 17 different states. The Belmullet part of the Scheme was overseen by Mr Sydney Buxton and Captain Ruttledge-Fair. According to his report, about 2,400 applied from Belmullet alone, while less than ten percent of them were selected.

The Heverons were one of ten families chosen from Doolough. On 22 June 1883, my great-grandparents, Philip and Mary Heveron, and their six children, one of them my grandmother, left Elly Bay in North Mayo on the *SS Waldensian* arriving into Boston Harbour on 4 July.

They were one of three families ticketed to Warren, Rhode Island where my great-grandfather, Philip Heveron, reported to the superintendent of Warren Manufacturing Company. They were given one of the mill-houses on the corner of North Water Street and Bowen which they shared with the Monaghan family.

The children went to the school nearby, the older ones may have worked in the mill; another child was born and baptised in St Mary's Church.

However, they couldn't settle and within 18 months they found their way back to Ireland. We have not been able to find any ships' records for their return journey but we know they arrived in Cobh in 1884. From documents in the Cork City and County Archives we learn that my great-grandmother and seven children were admitted to the workhouse on 10 November 1884.

There is no evidence that Philip Heveron was admitted which suggests that he went straight to Belmullet to find a home for them. Documents also state that the three youngest were in very poor condition. Young Margaret, who was about eight years of age, contracted phthisis, a form of TB, and died there in February 1885. We believe she has been buried in a mass grave somewhere.

They left the workhouse on 28 April 1885 to return to Belmullet. Philip no longer had land in Doolough and they joined the Gaughan's (his wife's family) nearby. Two more children were born. It wasn't until 1889 that they had their own holding again.

Still the land couldn't support them. There were yearly migrations to Scotland to pick potatoes. Some family members eventually settled there. My grandmother grew up and married Anthony Henry from Roy, Belmullet who supervised the potato picking. They, too, migrated back and forth. They had twelve children; my mother was born in Edinburgh on one of those migrations. Emigration continued into the next generations, and destinations included New York, Boston, London, Bedford, Edinburgh and Glasgow.

Their standard of living had eventually improved. Now there were chests of tea, sacks of flour, fiddles and bone china in their house.

My mother grew, married and I was born, the ninth of ten children. I, too married and we have a son and a daughter. In the way of it, the story has gone full circle. Migration continues in our family with our daughter, her American husband and children. Our grandchildren.

This poetry collection attempts to chart the course of my ancestors' leavetaking and homecoming through documented fact, images and memory in order to keep their story alive.

Bone Road

in word and image

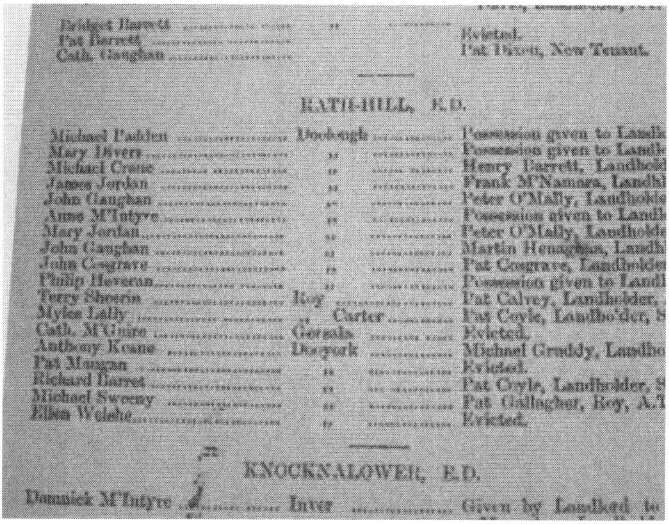

Bridget Barrett	„	
Pat Barrett		Evicted.
Cath. Gaughan		Pat Dixon, New Tenant.

RATH-HILL, E.D.

Michael Padden	Doohogh	Possession given to Landl
Mary Divers	„	Possession given to Landl
Michael Crane	„	Henry Barrett, Landhold
James Jordan	„	Frank M'Namara, Landh
John Gaughan	„	Peter O'Mally, Landhold
Anne M'Intyre	„	Possession given to Landl
Mary Jordan	„	Peter O'Mally, Landhold
John Gaughan	„	Martin Henaghan, Landh
John Cosgrave	„	Pat Cosgrave, Landholder
Philip Heveran	„	Possession given to Landl
Terry Sheerin	Roy	Pat Calvey, Landholder,
Myles Lally	„ Carter	Pat Coyle, Landholder, S
Cath. M'Guire	Geesala	Evicted.
Anthony Keane	Doopork	Michael Graddy, Landho
Pat Mangan	„	Evicted.
Richard Barret	„	Pat Coyle, Landholder, S
Michael Sweeny	„	Pat Gallagher, Roy, A.T
Ellen Welshe	„	Evicted.

KNOCKNALOWER, E.D.

Dominick M'Intyre	Inver	Given by Landlord to

Disposal of family holdings in Belmullet

from the Tuke Report

Hunger for Somewhere Else

They're glad to see the back
of all the wind-crippled whins,
turn their heads from
the rain over Achill head,
smoor the final fire.

They've had their bellyful
of stinking haulms,
grateful now to hand back
their hungry piece of grass to the landlord

and watch the dog on a scatter of stone,
a fetch in the tumbled-down *scailp,*
a fling of dunlins on sand
waiting for the boat to sail.

* *scailp*: earth hut or shelter under rock

SS Waldensian of the Allan Line

LEAVING

The longest day still entering their dawn,
they follow the carts of hopefuls,
along the famished track
down to the sea.

Beyond the calm waters of Elly Bay,
the *SS Waldensian* lies anchored,
brighter than any golden hoard
offered to Manannán, the sea god.

There are scant tears,
for their passage is paid;
new clothes on their backs,
landing money promised.

The whole family going:
my great-grandparents, six children,
ten-year-old Brigid, my grandmother
– that's Tuke's deal.

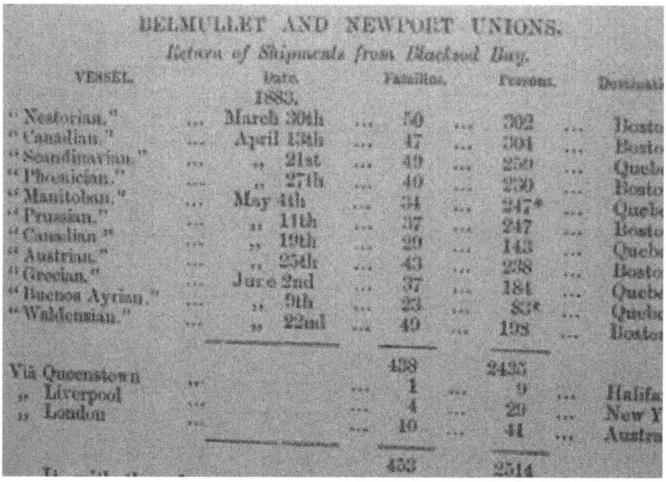

BELMULLET AND NEWPORT UNIONS.

Return of Shipments from Blacksod Bay.

VESSEL.	Date. 1883.	Families.	Persons.	Destinati
"Nestorian."	March 30th	50	302	Bosto
"Canadian."	April 13th	47	304	Bosto
"Scandinavian."	" 21st	49	259	Queb
"Phœnician."	" 27th	40	230	Bosto
"Manitoban."	May 4th	34	247*	Queb
"Prussian."	" 11th	37	247	Bosto
"Canadian."	" 19th	29	143	Queb
"Austrian."	" 25th	43	238	Bosto
"Grecian."	June 2nd	37	184	Queb
"Buenos Ayrian."	" 9th	23	83*	Queb
"Waldensian."	" 22nd	49	198	Bosto
		438	2435	
Via Queenstown		1	9	Halifa
" Liverpool		4	29	New Y
" London		10	41	Austra
		453	2514	

Belmullet and Newport destinations
from the Tuke Report

Outfitted

Waiting for high-water,
the chosen clusters
are ferried by the blue jackets
on the *Seahorse* gunboat.

They leave the bay

then out through
the Narrows of Achill
where the water runs
with unrelenting force.

They climb aboard the steamer,
men in forward, women aft.

Outfitted with a straw bed,
a pillow to lay their heads,
enough marine soap
to wash the whole of Erris
out of them.

A swell builds mid-Atlantic.
Through spume and spindrift, they sail,
fog too thick for soupers,
they sight an iceberg.

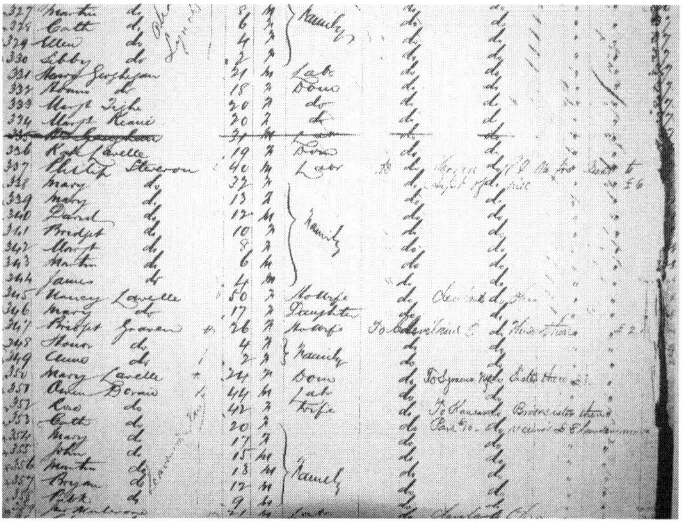

SS Waldensian's passenger manifest listing the family of Philip and Mary Heveron, 4 July 1883
(HS3.02/1990X, Massachusetts Archives, Boston, Massachusetts)

The Ship's Manifest

Philip Heveron
Mary Heveron
Mary Heveron
David Heveron
Brigid Heveron
Margaret Heveron
Martin Heveron
James Heveron

James Hack Tuke

WITNESS

'How patiently they bear their want'

When he got home to England,
he wrote to the papers.
Mr Tuke, merchant banker, Quaker,
told them how he had watched

a wraith sitting at a loom
with neither woof nor warp,
shunting the empty frame
forward, back

in a place where the poor sucked stones
from the road, ate their children's hair,
were blown like chaff
into the lake's unsated mouth.

And more failed years to follow,
rain that washed the turf back into the bog.
The best of them with nothing
but a mouthful of meal.

Clutches of begging letters sent to him
hidden under the wings of a hen,
and seeing what he saw
the only hope of their saving

was in the form of a fund
that sent the Allan Line
up and down the coast,
netting shoal after desperate shoal.

To Each Man

one suit of clothes
and to put inside that suit a shirt
and over that suit a coat
a handkerchief to stand proud
from the breast pocket
socks to soften his strong boots
a cap to keep the wind from his ears
a muffler to scarf him from the breeze
as he stands on deck
longing for the ocean to start

TO EACH WOMAN

a dress
and to set off that dress a jacket
a shawl to keep her shoulders warm
a bonnet to grace her hair
two sets of unmentionables
soft against her skin
stockings and a pair of boots
fine needles and thread
to bind her to the future

with her dirty *giobals* cast off
now she is all style
the new world will stand
in the snow to look at her

* *giobals*: old clothes, rags

D.—STATEMENT OF ACCOUNTS.

FIRST YEAR.—March, 1882, to March, 1883.

EXPENDITURE.	£	s.	d.	AVERAGE COST PER HEAD. (Exclusive of "Sundry Cases.") £	s.	d.
Ocean and Rail Fares	5,412	5	10	4	8	0
Clothing	1,200	3	3	0	19	6
Landing Money, or expended through Agents in America	466	11	11	0	7	·6
Conveyance and Lodging	644	15	0	0	10	6
Working Expenses	451	9	9	0	7	4
	8,175	5	9	6	12	10
Less received from Emigrants and private sources	745	16	8	0	12	1
Net Cost to Committee	£7,429	9	1	£6	0	9

BALANCE SHEET.

	£	s.	d.		£	s.	d.
By Subscriptions	15,794	19	3	To Net Expenditure supra)	7,429	9	1
				Sundry assisted cases ...	358	11	4
				Advertising, Printing, American travelling, and other expenses subsequent to Emigration	438	18	7
				Balance	7,568	0	3
	£15,794	19	3		£15,794	19	3

SECOND YEAR.—March to December 31, 1883.

TOTALS OF SEPARATE EXPENDITURE.	£	s.	d.	AVERAGE COST PER HEAD. £	s.	d.	
Ocean and Rail Fares... ...	21,418	19	2	4	0	0	
Clothing	6,352	10	10	1	3	3	
Landing Money	3,882	15	4	0	14	6	
Conveyance and Lodging ...	1,799	0	11	0	6	8	
Working Expenses	1,686	1	3	0	6	3	
	35,139	7	6	6	10	8	Or with General Expenditure, £6 13s. 9d.
Less Government Grants, and about £450 from Emigrants	26,867	12	4	5	0	0	
Net Cost to Committee ...	£8,271	15	2	£1	10	8	Or with General Ex-

Statement of accounts for 1882–1883 sailings
from the Tuke Report

some were sent to Fall River some were sent to Poughkeepsie some were sent to Passaic some were sent to Lost Creek some were sent to Wabasha some were sent to Minooka some were sent to Durango some were sent to Painsville some were sent to White Water some were sent to St Louis some were sent to Still Water some were sent to Dunlap some were sent to Winona some were sent to Pent Water some were sent to Woonsocket and North Water Street

What the New Settlers Saw

Once the people of the first light
tread gently here with their great chief
in the sheltered arm of Narragansett Bay.
They too had known plague:
all along Mount Hope Neck
was pocked with bones and souls
left for the buzzards to strip clean.

When the new settlers landed at Sowams
they saw only fieldful and swampful
of grape, of huckleberry,
water springing from white sands.
Rivers glistening with fish. Quahogs.

They wiped its true name from their lips.
Called it their own;
the one James Tuke knew it by
and centuries later sent my people to.

Why the Great Chief Gave the Settlers Land

Ancestors were coming for him.
He knew because the barred owl
screeched it from the full-dark tree.
Black-wolf's teeth were against his throat.
His eyes dead, but ears open
to the warriors that circled the bed,
pleading his spirit back.

When into this space of smoke and chant,
the whiff of white skin.
Settler Winslow placed the knife-tip
on the chief's parched tongue.
He tasted fruit, its juice. His eyes opened.

A pipkin of bruised corn, a slice of saxifrax root,
Winslow grinding them like a medicine man,
fed it to Massasoit, drop by quickening drop,
spooned the great sachem back to light.

Sowams to Warren

Called, not after the man
who saved the sachem's life

but the naval hero
with Irish links

whose fame in battle
let his name run

from broken red oak tree
to the narrows.

Warren town plaque

THIS MILL TOWN

A trading post,
blossomed into a town,
a whaling station,

and then the whales all gone,
no ambergris, no baleen, no oil
but cheap kerosene, coal

that grew the cotton mills.
Spindles flashed like lightening,
looms going hell for thunder.

A warren of streets overrun
by all the dispossessed.
Chimney stacks poked fingers at the sky.

ACCORDING TO *THE GLOBE*

Into Boston Harbour
on the Fourth of July,
flags cheering, firecracker boys,
speeches, brass bands,
my people come.
Eyes out on sticks with the welcome
they think is for them alone.

Their ticket says Water Street, Warren,
not far from the great sachem's spring.
The scent of trees, a house with stairs,
the likes they've never seen.

They start over in this town.
Within a week, steady work in the mill,
soon flesh on riddled bones,
shoes for the boys,
white bows in the girls' hair.

If the Dintys back in Doolough
could only see them now.

Warren waterfront with mill towers in the background

Beyond the Whale-Way

They step onto sidewalks
a word as alien as the thin sliver of sky
above their heads.
Water from a faucet not the dark mystery of well.

Newness walks around the street
on its own two feet,
willing to let go of elsewhere
forget the other that they have left behind.

Warren, Rhode Island, 1888, showing the towers of Warren Manufacturing Company in the background

Word Comes Back to Mr Tuke

Good families the letter says.
In fine fettle, happy with their lot,
even the children working in the mill.

Heverons and Monaghans
sharing on the corner
of Water and Bowen.

A stairway in their tenement
makes sure they are going
up in the world.

ON SEEING BROWN'S CASH GROCERY

for Diane Heveran Rothaar

First he must roll the word around in his mouth
to taste its hugeness as he stands and peers in the door
of John H. Brown's Mammoth Cash Grocery.

From here the new world bustles out its scent in greeting.
No part of him believes that dreams can be this real –
velvet skin of strange fruits, pelts of stranger animals.
Nine good cigars for twenty-five cents. Cinnamon.

With some of his landing cash still loyal to his pocket,
he sees how he might spend it on tea, on flour, salt or grain
but who in their right mind would spend it on blocks of ice,
or on *cipins,* when there are more trees here
than ten lifetimes ever saw back home.

And what about the earpiece, mouthpiece
clamped to the wall behind the counter?
If only there was its twin in Glencastle Post Office,
he would gladly hand over the last of his Tuke dollar,
crank up the Greek name for 'far' and 'sound'

and wait for that moment
when he would hear across the whale-road
the familiar cadence of home,
tell them that the worst meal here
was still better than the best one back there,
this new life sweeter
than the barrel of molasses he is standing by.

* *cipins:* kindling

John H. Brown's Mammoth Grocery

They Taste for the First Time

Bananas – eat them skin and all.
Who said bananas were nice?

But famine still in their bones
and if there are skins to be eaten,

there are skins to be eaten.
'Tell me the colour of your tongue', they say.

John Brown's Mammoth Grocery and Fulton's Market

Cotton

First the seed
the cream of flowers
pod becomes boll
dries, splits open,
curves back
to expose fibres.

Then the carding
    the drawn slivers
the ginning
    the roving
the sizing
    the spinning
the warping
    the slashing
the weaving
    the spooling.

Sheeting
shirting
sateen
twill
bolts of them
flowing
like rivers
into
Narragansett Bay.

Mill tower as it stands today in Warren, Rhode Island

Above their Station

November and they watch as winter flurries in,
a tracery of leaf, of fern, of crystal cave
etched across the frozen windowpane.

Mary heats her well-earned quarter in the candle flame,
lets the fire from the coin brand a perfect lens
on the frosted glass. A telescope
opening undiscovered worlds into the room.

She sees herself in a landau,
with its Moroccan leather and broadlace.
David, all swanky doodle dandy,
swanning up and down the thoroughfare.

And Brigid (my grandmother),
silk in her dress, silk in her hat
shading her too thin skin from snow and sun.

They lift little Martin up, and peering out
he can see no carriage wheels, no fancy silver cane,
just chimney stacks balling their fists at the sky.
His uproar has their father rushing in

who flays them with his ire,
for filling the child with lies;
his biting words chill their magic screen,
his rimed breath freezes their waking dream,
turns it icy white.

Water Street, Warren, 1890, looking south
where the Heverons and Monaghans lived

Grandmother as Girl

She's nowhere among the boys
with their left hands clasped
inside their jackets
as if keeping a scaldy warm,

nor along the line of white pinafores
over Sunday-going-to-mass dresses,
barely a half-smile shared between them
in the scratched and faded photo
taken that day in Warren Elementary.

I should know her from the picture
I have of her as a woman.
Is that her there, right there?
– centre front –

jut of jaw of the little one,
her arms crossed above her heart,
as if fearing the lens will steal
that part of her she most wants to hold onto.

As I scan the three rows of faces,
she's the only one
with that strong chin:
the purse of full-bottom lip

that had Haddon and Brown
rushing to the west of Ireland
with cameras, callipers,
head-hunting.

Cambell School, close to Warren Manufacturing Company

In Time he Realises

they have forsaken
one hunger for another,

mill work ten hours a day
six days a week, all year round

thousands of spindles
hundreds of looms,

waiting to snare a sleeve, an arm,
a tress of hair, lint choking lungs,

the tiniest stirrup of the ear
splintered by such noise.

The Carding Room of Warren Manufacturing Company, circa 1908 (WPS Meyer Collection)

He Longs for Bog Cotton

That lover of wet places,
some years there was so much of it,
its fruit transformed *puiteach*
into snow-covered tundra.

A counterpane of white above the bog,
picked to soften the inside of his shoes
when he walked to Belmullet on fair days,
flick of hare's-tail all along the sedge.

* *puiteach*: boggy ground, mud

Rain Over Achill

This night that is all moon –
its light playing puck with him
as he works his way home along Water Street
– spawns a silver river, a glister of fish.

His legs still think they are treadled
to the crank and shuttle of the loom,
the ache in his arms worse than
footing the whole of Doolough's turf.

For one startling moment, he doesn't see
the shingles of each single roof ahead.
Only the cap over Achill Head
when there was rain on it.

Water Street above Liberty Street looking south, early 1890s

Reflection

All this lunar night
the moon's cold seeps into
the emptied glass on the table
on the table itself
on his coat's shoulder
with a dander of lint
the row of small shoes
waiting by the door

where he sees

waiting by the door
the row of small shoes
with a dander of lint
on his coat's shoulder
on the table itself
the emptied glass on the table
the moon's cold seeps into
all this lunar night.

Going Back

Does it matter
whether it was the voice
that he heard that night
calling him out of the half-light,

or the blackbird on the steeple
(of the church just built)
singing its golden heart into the dawn
as he trudged his way to the mills,

but he bought a passage on a ship
still marked with famine
back to where the swan children
spent their last days,
where the barnacle geese
found their second home.

St Mary's Catholic Church, rebuilt 1883

Things to Do When you Go Home

Untumble the walls of the house.
Uprise its lintel from the overgrowth,
like a calf-skin psalter lifted from the bog.
Unlatch the door.

Unsmoor the fire.
Updraught the embers waiting there
all the while you were beyond the whale-way.
Untether its glow.

Unsour the fields.
Uproot the dock, the poison ragwort, scutch.
Ease the clay back in beneath your nails.
Unhang the rust-gnawed gate.

Unsay the words you felt you had to say
– upsticks – the leaving and the coming back.
Ring the rhyme of scythe along the day.
Unbreak the heart.

Forsaking Tuke's Future

There is a place beyond the dark
where the heart goes when it is drawn
further into a winter it is already in.

Not even two years gone, another child born,
they docked in Cobh, the workhouse,
forsaking Tuke's future.

Land, however blighted, was preferable
to all those factory stacks,
the clank and clatter of looms.

Streets just paved with streets, not the gold
of corn at saving time,
the saffron tint of whin,
mizzle over Erris that he thirsted for.

Hometown
for Maggie O'Brien

And what of the family who stayed
in the mill house on Water and Bowen,
the rooms they no longer shared?

They stayed,
eased into the loss of nine absent voices,
let other light find the lack of footfall on the stairs,
the dog of loneliness muzzled.

They stayed,
gave up each year's earnings to the grocer,
to keep as many mouths again fed,
shadows behind, faces to the sun.

They stayed,
stood on their corner street and watched
all three mills go up in flames. Looms to cinders,
spindles to ash, jobs to dust.

They stayed,
pulled themselves up from the hardscrabble,
births, marriages in St Mary's Church, it too rebuilt
from fire. Warren their home now.

They thrived.

Thomas Mona(g)han and his wife, Mary Ellen McKenna, Warren, Rhode Island, circa 1910. With his parents and 6 older brothers he shared the house on Water Street with the Heverons

By Design

How beautiful your drawings, how fine!
Indeed, masterful and ... for that price!
Pray tell me, Mr Wilkinson,
how you come to bear such
a skilled hand for one so young?

My father, sir, a builder in Whitney,
learned it all from him.
My first one standing in my hometown,
the next in Chipping North.
Eight of them up and running
by my twenty-second year.

How interesting, but at the outset let me tell you this,
I want no gaud, no frippery.
We are, as you know, ratepayers ourselves.
These Irish beggars cannot be choosers.
Let them eat scenery if they want pleasing.

I get your point, Commissioner,
and have planned for that. See here:
un-plastered walls, local stone-rubble,
each quoin and architrave hammer-dressed.
Floors of mortar and earth more suited to our guests
since it's what their bare feet are at home with, after all.

Well, Mr Wilkinson – George, if I may –
you have thought of everything. But ventilation!
Perfect calculations of fresh air per pauper!
Is that not stretching it a bit too far?
How can we control the numbers if fever
isn't let race through these structured flues
like wonder flows through summer?

But Commissioner, sir …

Above all else they must know their place.
Here there must be no lazy beds, no idle hands.

Commissioner, I have accounted for that just here –
the yard for breaking stones, for splitting oakum;
the yard for female idiots, the one for men,
and here in the comfort of this room they will swear
that they own neither kine nor cat, scrap nor scraw.

Such luxury, George,
you have planned for them a palace
the likes of which they've never known.
How in all that's good and holy
will we ever coax them to leave us?

Irish Workhouse Centre, Portumna, County Galway

Parting Promise

10 November 1884

He leaves them at the poorhouse gate,
their details entered by an exacting hand,
the bad condition they have landed in
ledgered in neat lines and columns.
His is the only one missing
– Philip Heveron, my great-grandfather.

Imagine that April parting promise
as something of him follows
the spoor of his yearning
back to the margin land he comes from,
where rain illuminates every broken field,
every lichened wall.

The dream holds him to the house
he will build near Shraigh National School,
his hands still able to read the shape of stone
and know the place
where he will build the hearth,
feel the weight of his heart against the one
where he will site their front door,
opening away from the wind to shelter them.

Cork workhouse arch, St Finbarr's Hospital grounds

The Arch

Through the hard-hip, well-rounded breast of the arch,
their bodies listing, they went.

The women ordered to turn left,
the boys right.

The weight of that ship on their backs,
the cold backwash of its eyes,

the way the streets of Warren
seeped out of their tight mouths,

sea streeled out from their hair.
Bones holding bones.

What could he have heard that night
that brought them back to this?

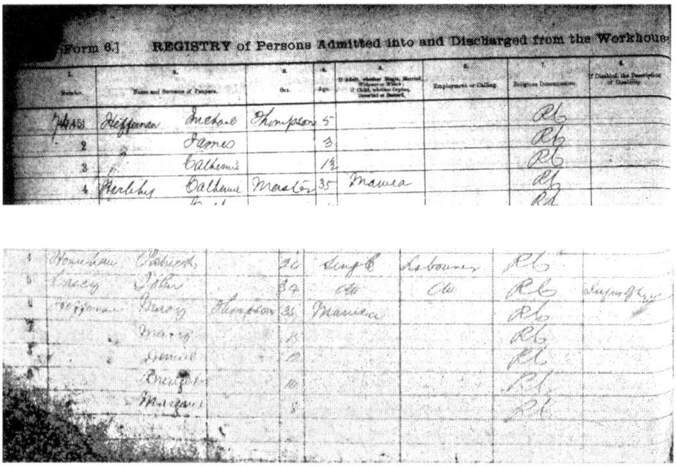
[Form 6.] REGISTRY of Persons Admitted into and Discharged from the Workhouse

Entry document to Cork workhouse

UNION WORKHOUSE

The saddest note in this place is the colour
that falls through holes in the roof,
as do the birds, their feathers and droppings

thick along the rafters into the space
where a rickle of bones walks
up and down between straw bundles.

The greening of voices echoes out of brick,
from ivy that grows along the windows,
hums itself into the corners of rooms
playing the notes over and over.

A child's hand stretches out just to know touch,
shoulders with blades, C sharp, that cut at will,
while the stars evicted from the sky
become ash blown from a dead fire.

What she Might Have Asked

We wait out each day, each week
for the few short minutes
when she hurries across the yard

as if it's Easter morning
and she wants to show us
the sun dance in the first sky.

She spit-wipes the dirt from our chins,
checks for spuds behind our ears.
We want to go home, mammy.

Did you say your grace before meals?

We did, gave thanks for the gifts of bounty,
blessed the hands that made the gruel.

Did you do your lessons? Break all the stones like they asked?

We show her nib-ink on our hands, grit in our palms.

We want to go home, mammy,
take us home.

Irish Workhouse Centre, Portumna, County Galway

Phthisis

i.m. Margaret Heveron; died in Cork workhouse February 1885

The word no longer used, the one she died of,
all the waves the ship had sailed across
had entered her before they'd docked in Cobh.

Ocean-flooded lungs, a bloodied cough,
with famished limbs, a fevered brow, they tossed
around the word no longer used, the one she died of.

In the women's yard, her mother could not move
the wall that kept her from her child, a cross
that nailed her since they'd docked in Cobh.

Outside the sickroom window, cold and rough,
they broke stones, the indigents, the dross
who feared to use the word, the one she died of.

A burning bush consumed her, as if God above
had sent Moses to her with its fire, its force
that flamed within her when they docked in Cobh.

To see another day the one thing that she'd love.
The cooling air upon her skin, gone all because
a word no longer used, the one she'd surely die of.

In a mass grave somewhere, no name to prove,
no way to mark her life, repair that loss.
The word no longer used, the one she died of,
remembered here, the day they docked in Cobh.

Irish Workhouse Centre, Portumna, County Galway

Starting Over

Which road they took
    to find their way back
is lost with them
    but they followed it
till they reached
    their thin bits of living
that they scrawb'd from
    the wind-whipped hollow land.
Erris in their marrow,
    the Mullet in their bones,
as crucial to them
    as breathing.

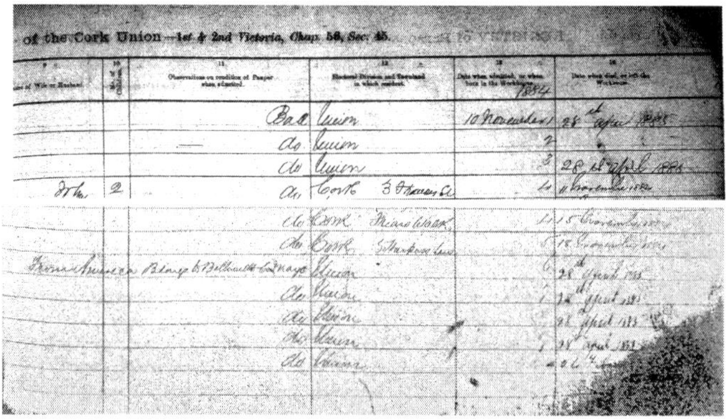
of the Cork Union — 1st & 2nd Victoria, Chap. 56, Sec. 45.

Discharge from Cork workhouse

BELMULLET THE TALK OF BYZANTIUM

This margin land –
no road in or out of it
until eighteen twenty-four –
was once known only from the sea.

On the orders of emperors
and guided by ancient maps,
seamen steered their boats
through the Bosphorus Strait,
the Aegean, battled the Atlantic roil
until they spied Broadhaven Stags,
their landmark and their goal
– the common whelk –

found only on this coast,
not common then
for when 'milked' its sluggish hue
turned imperial in the Erris air,
purple, so vibrant, it put to shame
the heather, loosestrife, vetch.

Worth its silver weight,
the prized last sliver on the spectrum of light,
this empyrean tint, was brought back,
brought down to earth
in the swish and trim of regal silks,
and while its colour trended,
made Belmullet
the talk of all Byzantium.

Original stone of Shraigh School from 1888

HOME

Morning doesn't break here,
not like over there where it split open
like an egg at the side of a bowl
and out spilled its glair, its brash yolky sun.

Here it breathes its best self into the light,
glints open the first blackbird's eye to sing,
shines through the kitchen window
to the slow hum of waking.

Slips the whole of the sky into its mouth,
holds onto it for all the hours
the new world beyond the ocean
is still in darkness, waiting.

MARGARET 1889

Another girl born
another child
given the dead's name

BLIGHTED

Your name came to you seaward
upon a ship returning home from Warren
where your family never settled.

Against the tide they travelled back
kept hidden in your mother's shawl that sick sister
until the poorhouse buried her.

When it was time to christen you
her ghost name was put to use again,
each of its letters blighted one by one.

You carried her weight on your back,
the flooded ocean of her eyes,
the way the stones of the workhouse
scraped against your crooked teeth.

You heard the cry of her along the lazy beds
as you barrowed swill to the pigs,
caught her on the slant of salt air,
your body listing.

The Missing Link

The head-hunters came
to the wildness of the west
in the eighteen nineties to prove
the natives' nigrescence, their blackness.

They lined the men up, full face, side view,
measured to a fraction of an inch –
forehead to crown, temple to temple,
the jut of the bone from ear to ear:

Seán 'the common noun' Daly,
the schoolmaster at Ballycroy,
the King of North Iniskea.

Women milling grain in the quern,
the purse of their full-bottom lip,
the protruding lower jaw.

If it wasn't for the white of their skin,
they'd be the living proof.

Jigging Up a Storm

They too took the boat – the spent clayspade of land
unable to feed those who came after –

back and forth to Scotland to pick potatoes.
Babies born on the winter stretch of migration.

My grandmother met a Henry from Roy
who found work with a seed merchant in Glasgow;

a ganger like others he returned
each season to recruit the Erris pickers

and when the boat docked at Pickle Point,
unloaded onto the pier chests of tea,

flour, bone china for his wife,
dresses for his four daughters,

fiddles for the eight boys, rosined
and ready to snatch a slow air

from the wind through bog cotton,
or jigging up a storm

that raised the rafters with
each perfect beat, out the open roof,

all the way down to the strand,
all the way over the waves.

Ayrshire potato season, Girvan, 1907
Anthony Henry, husband of Brigid Heveron, front right

Let Loose the Fire

for the Henrys

Hearts ripe for freedom, my uncles, mere boys,
boycotted school, never to return
when the Master called the Irish *savages*.

Choosing instead the three Rs:
rebel, rising, republic

learned from men whom they joined
at the day's dimming
or cycled by with a tip of their cap,

the blacksmith who forged their pikes,
taught them to make dummy rifles,
hid bullets in the frames of their bikes.

The GPO – as far from them as America –
they waited out the days for orders to filter down,
learned the art of taking cover;

then they could shake out
the spark from the ashes,
let loose the fire when their time came.

Michael Henry (born 1897, 1st child of 12
of Brigid Heveron and Anthony Henry)
on his wedding day to Eileen Coffey, Easter, 1949

Grandmother as Woman

Now she knows no want.
A plump of ducks in the yard,
sacks of flour by the dresser,
big enough to feed the village
when they come hungry to her door.

Lace cuffs at her wrists,
the fur collar of her coat
warming the pearls at her neck.

The pig killed at Martinmas,
and all but its squeal dished out.
And, with it, she hopes
the last traces of the pauper
have been cleaved from her.

Brigid Heveron, the author's grandmother

When they Said the Lord's Prayer

they thought
they were saying it
to their uncle

and so they implored
'Our Father
and Martin Heveron ...'

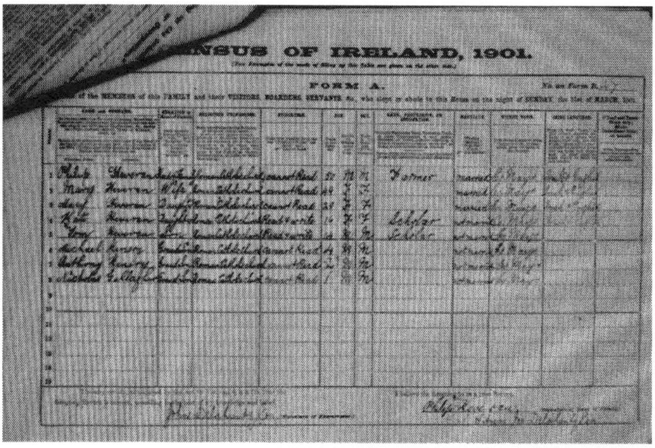

Census, 1901

Butter Stamp

for my grandmother, Brigid Heveron

Tuned to the turn of sound,
to the song of the churn,
my grandmother drew the dash
up and down the cream,
listening for the flecks of gild to form.

And then the butter came.

Washed and washed again, salted,
she slapped it into shape,
marked it with her stamp, the only solid thing
passed down from her to me.

Its grip burnished to sheen from all that use,
my hand folds over the honeyed wood,
where once her palm pressed it
into the golden round

leaving a perfect imprint of chevrons,
a cluster of strawberry leaves, its seeded fruit,
and in that way, overlaid
all that had gone before:
blight blossom, down-lying, poorhouse.

Brigid Heveron's butter stamp

Pearl

i.m. of my mother

The grit that found
its way in under her nail
turned the finger septic

as a young girl sent over
on the boat with her brothers
to toil the dark harvest,

pickers bent over like question marks,
knuckles skinned,
trawling the ridges for tubers

only fit for sleep
after bowls of what
she'd picked, boiled,

sleeping on straw in the women's bothy
to dream of gloves
with jewel buttons, necklaces.

What happened after that
is gone with her except the nail abscessed,
the bed of it infected;

no oyster way to mantle it layer over layer
of nacre, reverse its taint to lustre, pearl.
Instead, lanced and lanced again

it lost its memory to grow straight
but ridged and beaked like abalone
grew a further eighty years

among the perfect others of her right hand,
and funny how laying her out,
the undertaker painted it
mother-of-pearl, lustrous, reflecting light.

Annie M. Mills (née Henry),
the author's mother

LEGACY

for Geneviève and Daniel

My grandmother has come down
through me to you,
lives on in that same jut of your jaw,
that same full purse of lower lip.

Lives on in the family lore
that stops the snowblaze of whitethorn
before it reaches the Maytime threshold,
no new shoes on the kitchen table,
no vexing the fairies with dirty dishwater
nor knocking one small stone from their fort.

So, if I cross your sticky eye
with my gold of ring
or stem your bleeding knee
with ribwort chewed to poultice,
it is because it is the way it was shown to me,
as to my mother,
her mother
and her mother
before that.

Waiting for Our Grandchild

We are relearning lullabies,
take our old voices out of storage,
dusting off *angel, night-night, hush.*

The first scan of you on the fridge
is held there by magnets, as you are
to the pull of your father's heart,

your mother's – who comes back to visit us,
gravid with you. Sleeps in the old bed for the last time
where she was first whispered,

safe then within my heart, as you now within hers,
your fingers already formed, your lungs stronger,
your ear attuned to her voice.

She knows it is time to let go
of all her childhood things,
takes the faded posters from the wall

of moments when she shone:
Carousel, My Fair Lady, Miss Saigon,
ready for this new stage of mothering,

while your father dreams
in the too-long days of deployed duty
about when he gets back home,

of driving you both across
the wheat fields of North Dakota
golden as the hair on his two darlings' heads.

Bone Road

If my great-grandparents had not made
that journey back,
some other mother would have been born,
some other me. But they did

and now the pattern repeats itself,
not sea but air, not hunger but heart
that calls our daughter to upsticks,
follow the same whale-way.

This is no fairy story
I will tell our grandchildren
as they wave their spangled banners,
carry lineage in their eyes

of a man, a woman, their six children,
who, grateful for the passage paid,
left behind the bone road, took the boat,
grasped the hand of refuge

waiting for them on the other shore;
and that in-between time
saw their leavetaking
as the only way to find home.

ACKNOWLEDGEMENTS

I wish to thank:

The Arts Council for supporting this project with a Covid-19 Crisis Response Award

Galway County Council who awarded me an Individual Artists' Bursary Award in 2018 to work on this collection.

My deepest gratitude to:

Alan Hayes for his constant support and belief in my writing.

Diane Heveran Rothaar whose invaluable research on the family tree gave me many of the historical facts used here, including the postcard: Ayrshire potato season, Girvan, 1907.

Mary Kyne, Dr Gerard Moran, the Tuke Emigration Project Oughterard Committee and The Tuke Emigration Project Clifden Committee.

Rosemarie Geraghty of Blacksod Bay Emigration for her generous response to my various requests.

Lisa and Russ Taylor for their friendship and taking me to North Water Street in Warren, Rhode Island to see where my ancestors lived.

Philip Traynor and family for hosting the Heveron/Heveran Gathering of September 2017.

All my poet friends who kindly gave feedback on many of the poems: Hedy Gibbons-Lynott, James Martyn Joyce, Gerry

Hanberry, Siobhán Shine and Hugo Kelly, Susan Rich and Eamonn Wall.

The Tuke Report.

Within the Mullet by Rita Nolan where I read about Belmullet's connection with Byzantium, and *Massasoit's Town: Its History, Legends and Traditions* by Virginia Baker which documented the great sachem's connection with the settlers.

Jenny Corcoran for her expertise on the Great Hunger.

Charlotte Kelly for her perfect cover image.

My sisters and brother for their constant support.

An earlier version of 'Blighted' and 'Pearl' were first published in *Toil the Dark Harvest* (Bradshaw Books, 2004).

'Union Workhouse' was first published in *An Urgency of Stars* (Arlen House, 2010).

Orbis, Live Encounters, The Human Journal where early versions of these poems were first published.

Peter Moore, Galway, Ireland.

Mary Henry Kirwan, Tipperary, Ireland.

Maggie O'Brien, great-granddaughter of Patrick and Catherine Mona(g)han and granddaughter of their son, Thomas.

George Hail Library, Warren, Rhode Island, USA.

Irish Workhouse Centre, Portumna, County Galway, Ireland.

Massachusetts Archives, USA.

The Massasoit Historical Association of Warren, Rhode Island, USA.

Norwayheritage.com

Warren Preservation Society, Rhode Island, USA.

National Archives of Ireland.

Cork City and County Archives.

Last, but not least, my heart's best treasures, Peter, Geneviève and Daniel, Jenny, Jake, Lia and Lowen.

ABOUT THE AUTHOR

Geraldine Mills is a poet and fiction writer. Her first two collections of poetry, *Unearthing Your Own* (2001) and *Toil the Dark Harvest* (2004) were published by Bradshaw Books. Arlen House has published *An Urgency of Stars* (2010) and *The Other Side of Longing* (2011) as well as her three short story collections, *Lick of the Lizard* (2005), *The Weight of Feathers* (2007) and *Hellkite* (2013). *Gold*, her first children's novel, was published by Little Island in 2016. Her most recent poetry collection *Bone Road* was published by Arlen House in 2019.

She has won numerous awards and bursaries for her fiction and poetry including the Hennessy/*Sunday Tribune* New Irish Writer Award, a Patrick and Katherine Kavanagh Fellowship for *An Urgency of Stars* and she has been awarded two Arts Council bursaries. She collaborated with American poet, Lisa C. Taylor on the joint collection *The Other Side of Longing* which was chosen as the 2011 Gerson Reading at the University of Connecticut.

Her fiction and poetry are taught on contemporary literature courses in universities in St Louis, Missouri, Connecticut and Massachusetts, USA, and on the Emerson College summer course, County Clare.

She was awarded an Arts Council Covid 19 Crisis Response Award to work on a video representation of the poetry of *Bone Road*. She is a facilitator with Poetry Ireland's Writers in Schools' Scheme.

www.geraldinemillswriter.blogspot.com
@writergermills